Great Graphs in Ten Days

Written & Illustrated by B. K. Hixson

Use this Book, Please

The Required Legal Hoo Hah

Hoo Hah for Teachers

Teachers, please feel free to make copies of these ideas and use them in your classroom. That is why they are here. This also fulfills one of our objectives in life, which is to share as many cool, workable science and math ideas as we can. If you find the chief copy manager at your large and bureaucratic school district does not believe this page is valid, please have them contact us, and we will be happy to provide them with legal relief in the form of an oral confirmation… or, for the truly cautious, dare we say anal retentive, additional written permission.

However, we would kindly ask that you not make copies for all of the teachers in the school, your district, or the adjoining counties without securing our written permission first. This is not as hard as you might think if you are planning an in-house seminar. God forbid you take these ideas and improve the quality of education in an entire district. How would we sleep at night?

Have fun with the kids!

Table of Contents

A Note for Those Who Seek

... i.e. Teachers

This book has been designed to be used as a consumable lab book to teach your kids how to collect data, present it properly in a data table and then interpret the data as a graph of one kind or another. It is our intent that you spend about 35 to 45 minutes a day, for 10 consecutive days to achieve "Graph Master" status with all of your kids.

If you are a home school teacher the advice is pretty much the same. Your kids need to know how to collect data and present it in a clean, readable format that is easy to interpret. 10 days, 35 to 45 minutes a day is still our advice to you.

Abbreviated Lesson Plans

You will definitely get your own rhythm going after you teach this once or twice, but to shove you down the hill and get your rolling, may we suggest...

Week 1

Day 1	*Activities*	*Reference Page*	*Time allotted*
	Introduce the idea of Data	10	5 min
	Lab #1: Helicopters	12	25 min
	Helicopter Homework	14	15 min
Day 2			
	Review/Grade Helicopter Homework		10 min
	Introduce idea of a Tabulation Data Table		5 min
	Lab #2: Heads or Tails	15	20 min
	Heads or Tails Homework	17	10 min
Day 3			
	Review/Grade Heads or Tails Homework		10 min
	Lab #3: Conductivity Tester	18	25 min
	Conductivity Tester Pie Graph	21	10 min
Day 4			
	Review/Grade Conductivity Tester		10 min
	Reading Data Tables	22	5 min
	This Stuff Called Graph Paper	23	5 min
	Reading & Constructing Data Tables	24	15 min
Day 5			
	Review/Grade Reading & Constructing Data Tables		10 min
	Lab #4: Liquid Densities	31	25 min
	Questions and Graphs from Liquid Densities		10 min

to Enlighten the Next Generation

Week 2

Day 6			
	Review/Grade Liquid Densities		10 min
	Learning to Speak Line Graph	45	5 min
	Line Graphs in Reverse	34	25 min
Day 7			
	Review/Grade Line Graphs in Reverse		10 min
	Lab #5: Instant Handwarmer	36	25 min
	Instant Handwarmer	38	15 min
Day 8			
	Review/Grade Instant Handwarmer		10 min
	Lab #6: Pendulum Puzzles	39	25 min
	Pendulum Puzzles	42	15 min
Day 9			
	Review/Grade Pendulum Puzzles		10 min
	Vocabulary Test	43	15 min
	Review/Grade Vocabulary & Spelling Test		10 min
	Review for Exam as Class		15 min
Day 10			
	Final Exam	45	30 min
	Review/Grade Final Exam		15 min

Conferral of Graph Master Status (Certificates)

Answer Key

Sorry, that's against our religion ... seriously, if you made it through high school, enrolled in your first year of junior college or even thought about getting your Bachelor's degree you won't need us to tell you the answers to these questions.

However, in the event of a major brain cramp, you can always give us a call on our toll free number, 888-403-1189 and we will be happy to walk you through any problems that you may be having. And yes, if you insist, we will even tell you the answers.

Grading the Lab Activities/Exams

On the next two pages you will find a student grade sheet. Under each gradable item you will find the suggested breakdown for HOW to grade that item. This is only a guide and not is intended to insult the intelligence, integrity or professionalism of graphing specialists and educators anywhere.

Assignment/Grade Sheet

Day	*Due Date*	*Assignment*	*Reference Page*	*Points*
1	________	Helicopters Q 1-7: 1 point for each answer Q 8: 2 points for answer	14	___/15
2	________	Heads or Tails 2 points for each space	17	___/20

3	________	Conductivity Pie Graph
		Page 20 (5 points)
		    1 point of each blank
		Page 21 (10 points)
		    2 points for the title
		    2 points for the dividing line
		    2 points for shading insulators
		    2 points for labeling conductors
		    2 points for labeling insulators
			21	___/15

4	________	Reading & Constructing Data Tables
		Page 25 Q1 (10 points)
		    2 points for each part of the data table
		Page 25 Q 2 (10 Points)
		    1 point for each blank
		Page 26 Q3 (10 points)
		    1 point for the title
		    1 point for each variable (2 pts)
		    1 point for each unit (2 pts)
		    1 point for each ordered pair (5pts)
		Page 26 Q4 (10 points)
		    1 point for the title
		    1 point for each variable (2 pts)
		    1 point for each unit (2 pts)
		    1 point for each ordered pair (5pts)
			24	___/40

5	________	Liquid Densities
		Page 33 (20 points)
		    1 point for each box filled in properly
		Page 35 (20 points)
		    1 point for the horizontal axis
		    1 point for the vertical axis
		    1 point for the title
		    2 points for variable (unit) (2 pts)
		    1 point for each liquid (5 pts)
		    2 points for each bar (10 pts)
			31	___/40

Day	*Due Date*	*Assignment*	*Reference Page*	*Points*
6	________	Line Graphs in Reverse	34	___/24
		Page 35 Q1 (12 points)		
		1 point for each blank, A – E		
		$^1/_2$ point for each ordered pair		
		Page 35 Q2 (12 points)		
		1 point for the title		
		1 point for each variable (2 pts)		
		1 point for each unit (2 pts)		
		$^1/_2$ point for each ordered pair (7 pts)		
7	________	Instant Handwarmer	38	___/56
		Page 37 Q1 (10 points)		
		1 point for each blank, A – E		
		$^1/_2$ point for each ordered pair (5 points)		
		Page 37 Q2 (14 points)		
		2 points for the title		
		2 points for each variable (4 pts)		
		2 points for each unit (4 pts)		
		2 points for ordered pairs		
		2 points for a neat set of boxes		
		Page 38 (32 points)		
		2 points for the title		
		2 points for each variable (4 pts)		
		2 points for each unit (4 pts)		
		2 points for ordered pairs (20 points)		
		2 points for a neat line		
8	________	Pendulum Puzzles	42	___/55
		Page 41 (15 points)		
		1 point for each blank in the data table		
		Page 38 (40 points)		
		2 points for the title		
		2 points for each variable (4 pts)		
		2 points for each unit (4 pts)		
		8 points for each line (24 points)		
9	________	Vocabulary & Spelling	43	___/50
10	________	Final Exam	45	___/100
		Final Point Total/Grade		____/415 = ____

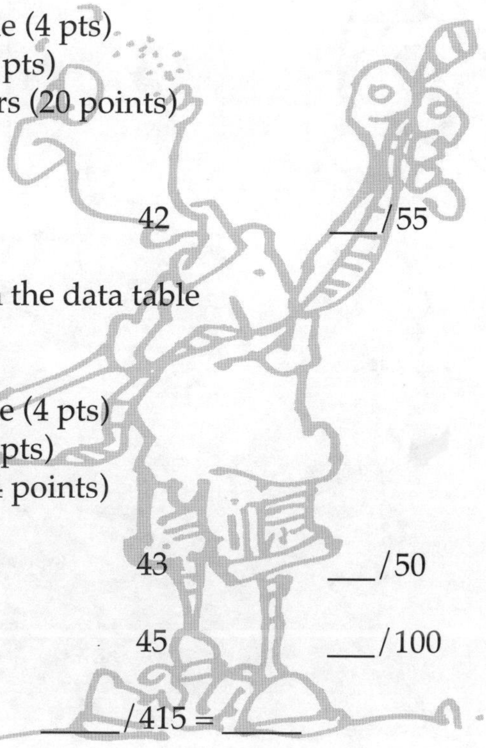

Holy Cow!

(Student)

We Were Mooved by Your Ability to Create Incredible Graphs

(Teacher/Principal) Date

Got an Eye Out for Someone With Exceptional Graphing Skills?

(Student)

Has What You're Lookin' For.

(Teacher/Principal) Date

The Labs, The Exercises, & A Couple of Exams

Data

What is Data?

Data is information—pictures, recordings, collections, drawings, notes—but most of the time it will be a big pile of numbers.

What Does It Look Like?

Numbers. Lots of numbers. We start with this because scientists most commonly collect and represent data using numbers. This is the kind of data that you will be looking to chase down most of the time. Whole numbers, numbers followed by decimals, positive numbers and negative numbers, lots of numbers with units behind them … all these types of numbers provide us with important information.

What Does It Tell Me?

Physical measurements tell you all kinds of things, such as how hot it is, how cold it might get, the amount of force needed to move an object, how tall the bean plants have grown since Jack planted them two days ago, and many others. These types of things all provide ***quantitative information***, which gives you specific details in the form of numbers. Another way of thinking of physical measurements is that they tell you how much of something there is—how much it weighs, how long it measures, how much it heats up, how much space it occupies, how fast it is traveling, or which note was produced when it squealed.

How Do I Collect This Data?

You must always collect measurements using the appropriate ***instrument***. If you are collecting weather data, you will want to use thermometers, anemometers, barometers, or hygrometers. If you are measuring mass, you may use a spring balance, triple beam balance, simple pan balance, or atomic scale. Length is measured using rulers marked in either English units, metric units, or both. Volume is collected using beakers, flasks, graduated cylinders, and pipettes, which give measurements in metric or English units.

What's the Big Deal?

Oh, nothing really. Graphing just makes life easier and decision-making a little quicker. There are basically two reasons that you should not only learn how to construct data tables and use graphs, but also incorporate them into your study of science: Organization and interpretation.

1. Organization

As a scientist, athlete, aspiring weather forecaster, doctor, mechanic, or whatever you decide to be, you are more than likely to be swamped with data. How much force was applied, how many free throws is she making, what is the current barometric pressure, how high is the cholesterol count, what is the pulling capacity of the motor in torque pound feet—these are all questions that require data to be provided.

A little bit of data is fine, but what happens if you request or collect data for several weeks or years? You are in for a numerical brain cramp that will cause your upper lip to involuntarily curl and your eyebrows to spontaneously fuse. To avert this social faux pas and impending neolithic disaster, you are going to need a way to organize the information. That's where data tables and graphs come in.

Data tables and graphs give you a structure, like see-through cabinets, to store and organize your data so that you can find it easily and refer to it quickly. Once data is organized, it is right there when you need to answer a question, prove a point, or double-check a fact. This is the first step in being able to use data correctly.

2. Interpretation

This is one of the main reasons that we collect and graph data. Numbers are nice because they are exact and informative, but if you need to make a quick decision, plotting all of those individual numbers into a single, quick-to-review picture allows you to interpret the data with ease. This helps you make decisions quickly and with confidence.

For example, everyone has seen those made-for-television hospital shows. Inevitably, they show a scene in a room where a patient is hooked to a life support monitor that tracks heartbeats. This monitor is constantly collecting, storing, organizing, and presenting this data as a line graph. The doctor can look at the line and instantly interpret the pile of data points and make a decision without having to look at each data point (single heartbeat) individually.

A lot of times, folks look at data tables and graphs not because they are trying to save someone's life but because they are making decisions about which product sells well for their company, how efficient a new airplane wing design appears to be, or whether or not the number of dogs loose in the neighborhood explains the sudden upswing in puppy chow sales. The point is that a graph is a picture of the data that has been collected. It allows you to quickly and efficiently analyze your data and, if necessary, draw a conclusion that you can act on. Now you know why it helps to build data tables and draw graphs.

Helicopters

Timeline
20-30 minutes

Vocabulary Builder
1. Data
Information that you collect during your lab.

2. Quantitative Measurement
The collection of data using calibrated instruments like beakers, rulers, and balances.

Concepts
The Need to Organize Data

The Experiment
You will cut a piece of paper and fold it into a design that twirls to the ground like a helicopter. After the initial *"ooh, aah,"* you can then very easily take this idea and produce a myriad of variations on this basic design.

Materials
1 Pair of scissors
1 Piece of paper

Procedure
1. Use the pattern on the next page as a template to be traced onto the piece of paper. Cut the design out along the perimeter and save the extra paper for additional projects.

2. Cut along the dashed lines. Once these cuts are made, fold one of the long strips (A) toward you, creasing it along the solid line, and the other (B) away from you. These are the rotors of the helicopter, and at this point, it should look like a giant capital *I* with bunny ears.

3. Fold the sides (C & D) into the middle just like you would fold a letter. This is the body of the helicopter.

4. The last thing to do is to fold the bottom (E) of the helicopter up about a half an inch. This fold helps keep everything together. A cartoon of what the final contraption should look like is shown on the next page.

5. Assume the helicopter flying position: Stand on the chair, extend the arm with the helicopter straight out into the air, and place your other hand on your hip. Drop said invention from outstretched arm. Make appropriate *"ooh, aah"* noises.

6. Now that the excitement has subsided, drop the helicopter again and estimate the amount of time in seconds that it takes to hit the floor once it leaves your hands.

7. Pick the helicopter up, measure 2 cm from the tip of each rotor, and snip the paper off the rotor. In effect, you are shortening the rotor and reducing the surface area pushing against the air in the room.

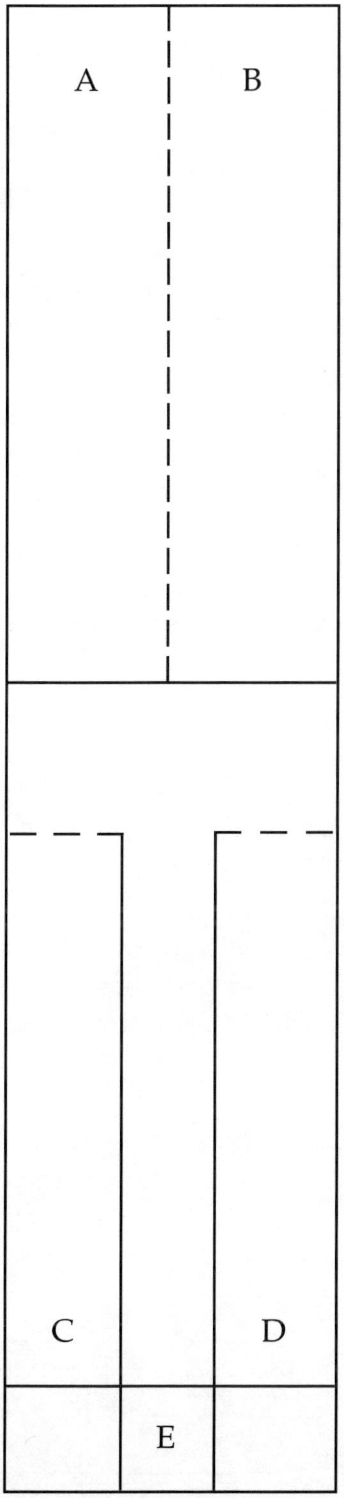

8. Drop the helicopter from the same exact height as in your first trial and reestimate the amount of time that it takes for the helicopter to hit the floor.

9. Snip another 2 cm from the tip of each rotor so that each is 6 cm long. Drop and record the amount of time it takes for it to hit the floor. Continue to shorten the rotors by 2 cm each time and record the time that it takes to fall to the floor.

How Come, Huh?

This is a simple exercise in air friction. As the helicopter falls to the floor, the air molecules push up against the blades and slow the descent. It spins because the blades are on opposite sides, causing unbalanced forces that spin the 'copter, resisting the fall, so that the rotors spin faster.

We started you out with this lab for one simple reason: To demonstrate the need for a way to organize the data that you collect. This lab was a lot of fun, you had some laughs, but the whole point of doing a lab is to make sense out of the data that you collect. And in this case, we didn't collect any data. We had fun but didn't come away with the most important part of doing a lab, *the data*, and that is the point of this whole 1 day exercise. To get you to a point where you are proficient at collecting, organizing, and depicting data so that you can use it.

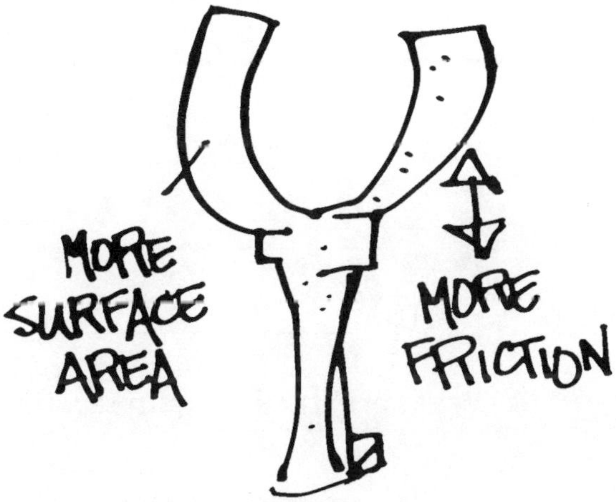

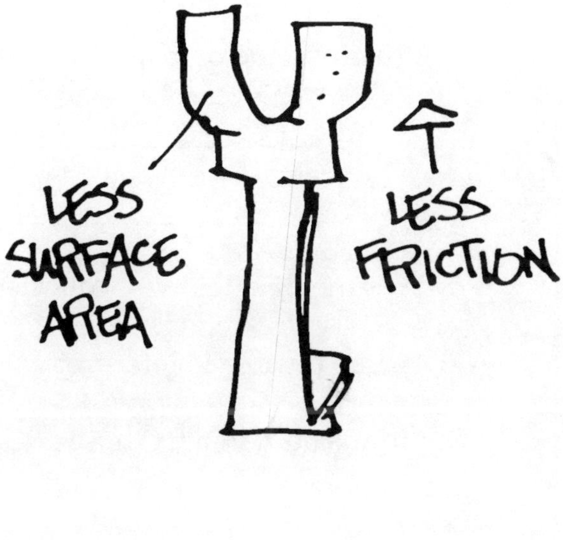

Name: ______________________ Assignment #1 Due: __________

Teacher: ______________________ Period: ________ Score: ____ /15 pts

Helicopters

Questions

1. Fill in the blank. Data is ________________________________.

2. What kind of information does data give me? ________________________.

3. List at least five different ways that data can be collected.

   A. ________________________________

   B. ________________________________

   C. ________________________________

   D. ________________________________

   E. ________________________________

4. What are the two main reasons that scientists use data tables and graphs?

   A. ________________________________

   B. ________________________________

5. What was the data that was being collected in the Helicopter experiment?

   A. ________________________________

   B. ________________________________

6. Was the data that you collected organized in any way? ______________

7. Were you able to interpret your data and determine any patterns? ____________

8. How would you fix those two problems? ________________________________

____

Heads or Tails

Tabulation Data Tables

So, lete's start organizing. Tabulation data tables allow you to collect and organize large samples of data based on one or a couple of variables. Typically, the information you want to remember can be recorded in a column using tally marks. Tables are typically aligned in a horizontal plane.

All data tables allow you the opportunity to record data in an organized manner. Because the data is recorded in an organized fashion, it is easy to locate and compare specific pieces of data. In this lab you have a quick reference to how many times the coin turned up heads and how many times it came up tails.

The Experiment

When you flip a penny into the air a hundred times, probability tells us that it will most likely land heads up half the time and tails up half the time. When you spin a penny a hundred times, you get an entirely different result. What comes up more often, heads or tails, and why?

Fortunately, it's lab time and time for an introduction to tabulation data tables.

Materials

1 New, Lincoln head penny
1 Hard surface
1 Pencil
Very good record keeping

Procedure

1. Construct two tabulation data tables or use the examples that we provide for you on page 48.

2. Spin the penny on a hard surface. When the penny comes to rest, place a tally mark in the appropriate row, heads or tails, depending on how the penny landed.

3. Spin the penny 100 times. Continuing to use tally marks, record the number of heads and the number of tails that you get each time. Bundle your marks in groups of 5.

4. Now, flip the penny 100 times in the air and catch the coin each time. Record your observations in the second data table.

Timeline

25-30 minutes

Vocabulary Builder

3. *Data Table*
An organized box where you enter the data that you collect during the experiment.

4. *Title*
A word or words that describes the data recorded in the data table.

5. *Column Header*
A word describing the kind of data recorded in that column or row.

Concepts

Tabulation Data Table

Heads or Tails

What Do Tabulation Data Tables Look Like?

They have a title, list two or more choices, and tally marks are used to record the results of the experiment or opinions of the survey. They are typically horizontal.

How Do I Make One?

All data tables have the following components:

A. **Title.** This describes the information that is being entered into the data table. Without the descriptive title, it is entirely possible that readers might not even know what it is that they are looking at.

B. **Column Header.** This is a word that describes the data that is being collected and the choices or options that are presented.

C. **Boxes.** If you are going to herd sheep, you need a corral. In science, we herd and organize data within vertical and horizontal lines that form boxes and keep the data where it should be.

What Do They Tell Me?

Tabulation data tables are generally used to **record opinions or choices**. This kind of data table does not necessarily need a constant. It can be used to record such things as the favorite fruit, from a choice of 5, among a group of kids, the results of a coin toss over a sample of 100 tosses, or your friends' favorite movie from a choice of 10 top-grossing movies this year. The data table containing a series of tally marks allows you to quickly look at the marks and see who is ahead.

How Come, Huh?

If you examine the penny carefully, you will notice that the side that shows Lincoln's head sticks out a little and has just a bit more metal on it than the other side. This extra mass on one side has an effect on a rotating object. It creates a force called torque.

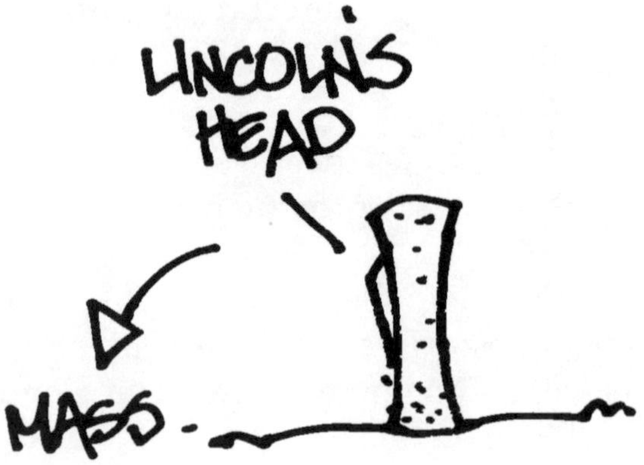

This torque, mild as it may be in this situation, affects the end result. You can see from the illustration shown here that it pushes the penny toward the heads side. This is something that should be supported by your data.

When you flip the penny into the air, the difference in mass becomes negligible and has little to no effect. Now, it simply becomes a matter of chance. Mathematical probability tells us that, if left up to chance, the penny will come up heads half the time and tails the other half. Is this what happened when you experimented? Review your data table to check.

Heads or Tails

Name: ______________________________	Assignment #2	Due: ____________
Teacher: ____________________________	Period: __________	Score: ____ / 20 pts

Prepare and Fill in the Data Tables below

All data tables have the following components:

A. **Title.** This describes the information that is being entered into the data table. Without the descriptive title, it is entirely possible that readers might not even know what it is that they are looking at. For our two data tables, we can use the following descriptive titles:

i. **Penny Spin, Heads or Tails**

ii. **Penny Flip, Heads or Tails**

B. **Variables.** This is a word that describes the data that is being collected and the choices or options that are presented. In this lab your choices are heads and tails.

C. **Boxes.** If you are going to herd sheep, you need a corral. In science, we herd and organize data within vertical and horizontal lines that form boxes and keep the data where it should be.

D. **Data.** In this case, the tally marks while you were doing the lab activity.

Ai.____

B.	D.
B.	D.

Aii.____

B.	D.
B.	D.

Pie Graph • Conductivity Tester

Timeline
25-30 minutes

Vocabulary Builder
6. Pie Graph

A picture of the data that has been collected represented as a circle or pie cut into portions. Each portion represents a group of the data collected.

Concepts
Tabulation Data Tables
Pie Graphs

Homework
Page 36. Due next class.

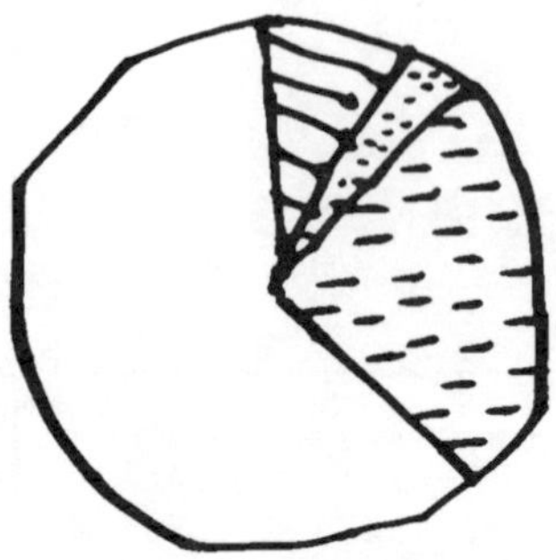

PIE GRAPH

Pie Graphs
These are round, just as you would expect from a pie. All of the data is divided from a whole, which is 100%. Each category is given an appropriately sized slice of the pie, and that category is usually identified by name and percentage.

For example, 100 people are interviewed and 42 say beef is their favorite protein, 30 say they like chicken because everything else tastes just like it anyway, 12 like pork, 10 prefer seafood, 6 think lamb is best, while 2 choose to suck down slices of tofu to get their daily intake of protein. A pie graph of that survey is pictured at the bottom left-hand side of the page.

The Experiment
Electrons are found in every atom. They are knocked loose and are bumped around all the time, but they do not have the ability to pass through all materials. In fact, they don't travel very well at all in materials called insulators. The materials that do allow electrons to zip on through are called conductors. This lab will introduce you to a technique that will allow you to test any material and determine if it is a conductor or an insulator. You will also use this experiment as an opportunity to make a new data table as well as construct a pie graph.

Materials
1 Battery with battery holder
1 Lamp with socket
3 Alligator clips
1 Nail, 8 penny
1 Copper wire, 18 gauge, 3 inches
1 Craft stick
1 Strip of fabric, 1 inch by 4 inches
1 Glass microscope slide
1 Plastic straw
1 Paper clip
1 Buzzer

Procedure
1. Snap the battery into the battery holder. Bend out the tabs on the ends of the clip so the alligator clips can be attached easily.

2. Assemble the circuit pictured below and to the right and make sure that the bulb lights up when everything is connected together.

3. Separate the two alligator clips (point A in the circuit) and test the nail by clipping it between the two alligator clips that you just separated. If the light goes on, that particular item is a conductor; if it remains unlit, it is an insulator.

4. Test each of the items in the data table one at a time by clipping them into the circuit. Mark the appropriate box in the data table below for each test.

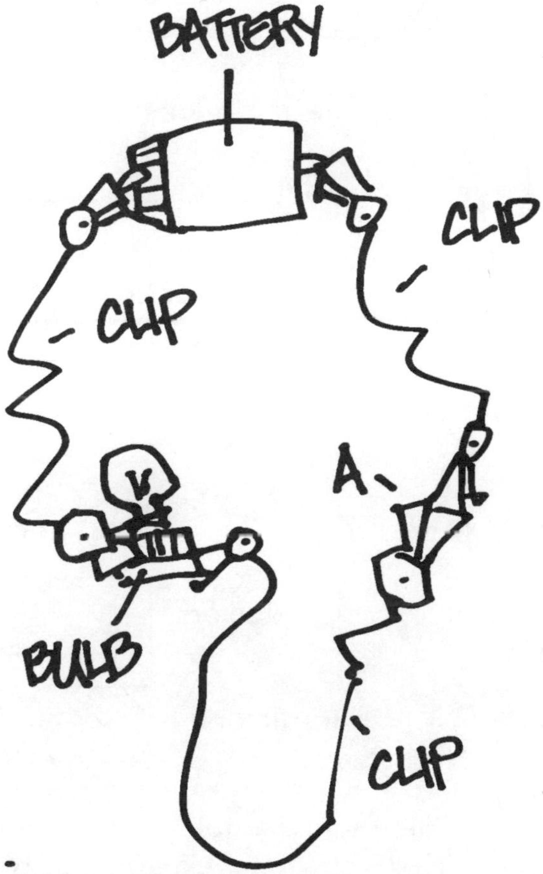

Data & Observations

Mark whether each is an insulator or a conductor:

Item	Conductor	Insulator
Nail		
Copper Wire		
Craft Stick		
Buzzer		
Fabric		
Microscope Slide		
Plastic Straw		
Lamp with Socket		
Alligator Clip		
Paper Clip		

How Come, Huh?

What you should have discovered is that metal objects make excellent conductors, while objects made of wood, glass, plastic, fabric, and other kinds of materials do not.

The main difference between these two is that the metals have a very orderly, simple, crystalline structure, whereas the others have more complex arrangements of molecules. The simplicity of the design for metals allows the electrons to flow freely through them, passing from atom to atom.

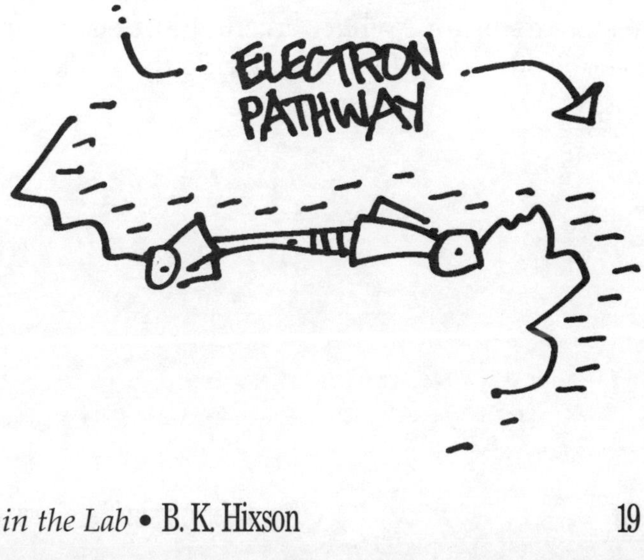

Pie Graph • Conductivity Tester

Creating a Pie Graph

A complete pie graph has four characteristics:

_____ A. A descriptive title.

_____ B. A big circle divided into percentage pieces. In this case you will sample 10 items, so each item represents 10% of the sample.

_____ C. Data, as pie pieces, identified.

_____ D. A key to identify the data. See bottom left hand corner on next page.

Using the information in this lab, fill in the blanks:

A. Title: ______________________________________

B. Data Collected

\# of conductors is _____ x 10% = ________ %

\# of insulators is _____ x 10% = ________ %

C. Key for Data

Conductors [ ]

Insulators [hatched box]

Here is an example of a pie graph that is set up and ready for you to fill in for this experiment. Of the 10 samples that you tested, determine what percentage of insulators and conductors were in the sample. Then divide the circle to the right accordingly.

Pie Graph • Conductivity Tester

Name: ______________________ Assignment #3 Due: __________

Teacher: ______________________ Period: ________ Score: ____ / 15 pts

____

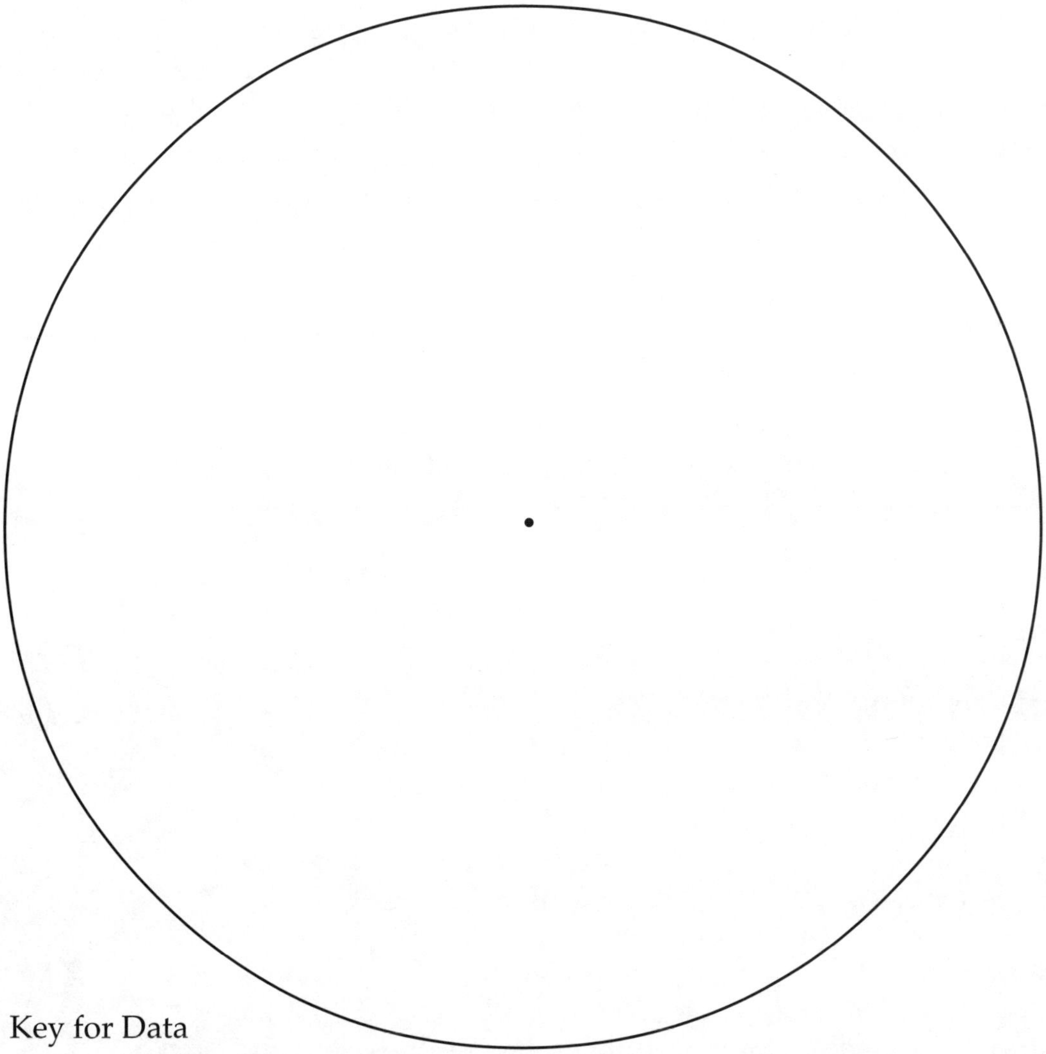

Key for Data

Conductors

Insulators

Reading Data Tables

What Do Complete Data Tables Look Like?

A complete data table has six characteristics:

A. A descriptive title.
B. A constant (uniform standard of measure).
C. Variable describing what information is to be collected during the experiment.
D. Units identifying how the variable and constant were measured, in parenthesis.
E. Data that has been collected in ordered pairs.
F. All data herded into neat, little boxes.

Here is an example of a completed data table measuring the temperature of water while it heats to boiling.

A.

B. **Heating of Ice Water** E.

Time (minutes)	0	2	4	6	8	10	12	14	16	18	20	22	24
Temp. (°C)	0	0	0	4	16	28	42	56	68	81	96	100	100

C. F.

D.

What Do The Parts of the Data Table Tell Me?

A. The Title

The title, Heating of Ice Water, pretty much lays it on the line. The lab is about the heating of water that is probably pretty cold at the beginning of the lab. A good title takes all of the guesswork out of identifying what the data in the data table describes.

B. The Constant

When you look at the data table, you see two sets of data, time and temperature. If you look more carefully at the numbers, you will notice that the time readings are very consistent, every two minutes to be exact. The temperature readings, however, are all over the place. Time is called the constant in this case. It is very predictable, it is consistent, it is even. It is the base that we use to let us know when to take the temperature readings. It tells us when to collect the data on the variable being tested.

C. The Variable

The temperature readings in this example are called the variable. The reason for this is that you have no idea what the readings will be until you take them. Unlike the time, which will have advanced two minutes each time you take a reading, the temperature is irregular. Sometimes it does not change at all and sometimes there are huge jumps in temperature. It varies.

Typically, in an experiment, the variable is the thing that you are testing. It is what you want to know. How does the temperature increase, how many swings will the pendulum make, what is the average rainfall? Those are variables.

D. Units

You will notice that behind the time constant is the word *minutes* in parentheses. Behind the temperature reading is (°C) for Celsius. These are the units of measure for the variable and constant. They tell you how the time and temperature are going to be measured—in minutes, seconds, or hours, (or) in Celsius, Fahrenheit, or Kelvin. Without the units, you do not know how the variable and constant were measured, and the data is worthless to you.

E. Ordered Pairs

Take a peek at the data table and you will also notice that there are pairs of corresponding numbers. At 16 minutes, the temperature was 68° Celsius. Those two numbers, taken together, are called an ordered pair. Every set of numbers in a data table is an ordered pair. These pairs are really easy to pick out because they are either side by side or one atop the other.

F. Boxes

Gotta keep the sheep in the pen. The boxes make the data table look neat and presentable and make it easier to follow and interpret the data and check facts.

How Many Kinds of Data Tables are There?

You will only be asked to make three different kinds of data tables: Tabulation, single variable, and multiple variable. We will go over each one, one at a time.

This Stuff Called Graph Paper

When you create data tables or graphs you will use a special kind of lined paper called, oddly enough, graph or graphing paper. Here are a couple of do's and don'ts when using graph paper.

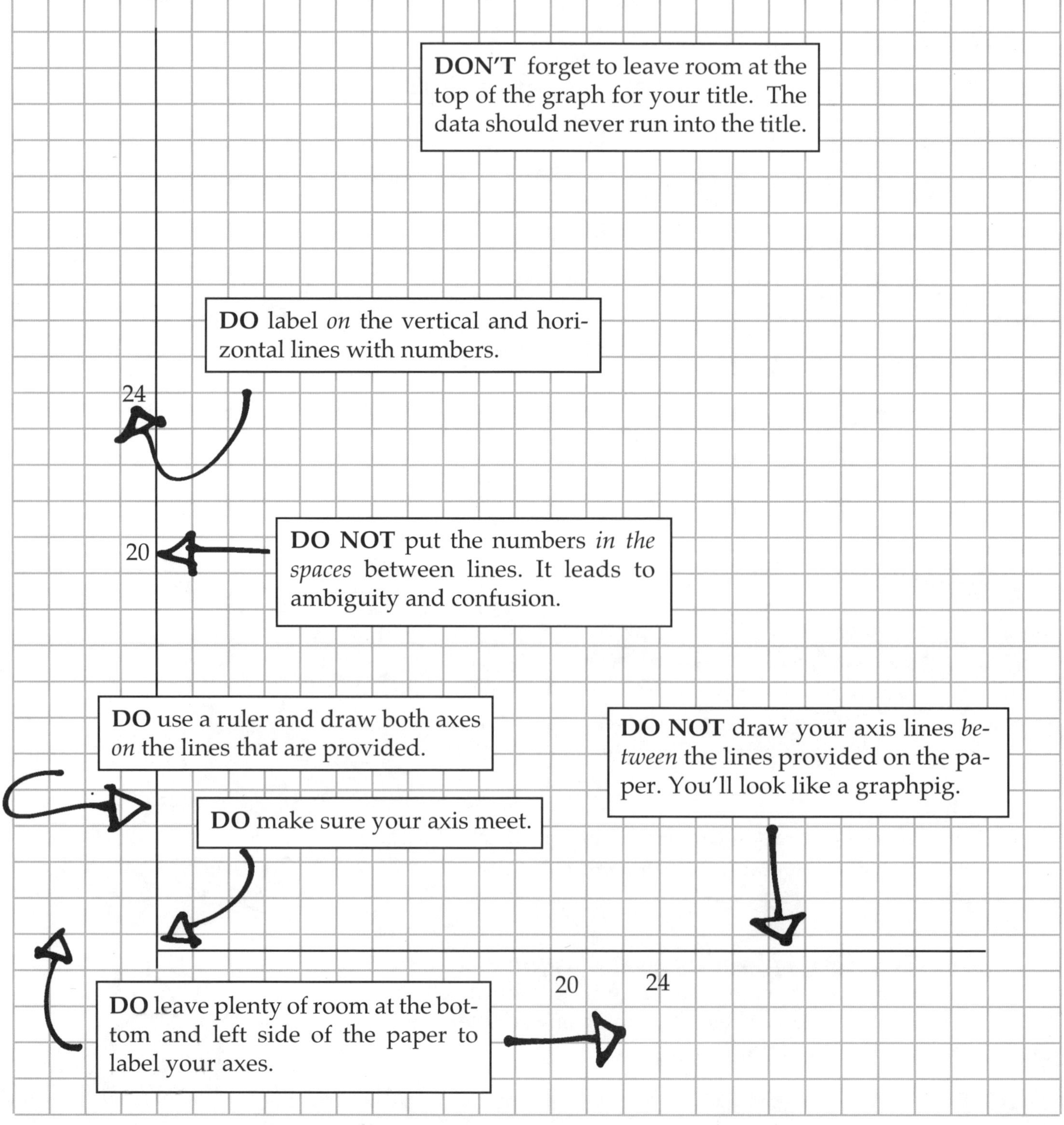

Reading & Constructing Data Tables

Name: ______________________ Assignment #4 Due: __________

Teacher: ______________________ Period: ________ Score: ____ / 40 pts

Follow the Directions

1. Using the data table below, correctly identify each part of the data table (title, constant, variable, units, data in ordered pairs, and boxes) and write the correct name on the line that points to that part.

Distance Rolled for a Metal Sphere

Distance rolled (centimeters)	0	6	22	45	68
Time (seconds)	0	2	4	6	8

2. Using the data table above, fill in the spaces below.

A. Title: ______________________________

B. Constant: ______________________________

C. Unit for Contant: ______________________________

D. Variable: ______________________________

E. Unit for Variable: ______________________________

F. Ordered Pairs: ______, ______ ______, ______

______, ______ ______, ______

______, ______

Reading & Constructing Data Tables

3. Using the information listed below, construct a data table in the space provided. In this lab a marble was rolled down an inclined ramp. The marble was allowed to roll until it came to a rest. The height of the ramp was increased each time. All data was collected in the order that it is presented below.

Rolling Marbles for Distance
Ramp height measured in centimeters is listed below.
0 cm, 5 cm, 10 cm, 15 cm, 20 cm, and 25 cm
Distance measured in centimeters, is listed below.
0 cm, 17 cm, 35, cm, 51 cm, 65 cm, and 72 cm

4. Using the information listed below, construct a data table in the space below. In this lab a liquid was heated until it boiled. All data was collected in the order that it is presented below.

Heating of Compound XJ–007
Time in minutes is listed below
0 min, 5 min, 10 min, 15 min, and 20 min.
Temperature measured in degrees celcius is listed below.
0° C, 12 ° C, 35 ° C, 86° C, and 153 ° C

Bar Graph • Liquid Densities

Bar Graphs

These are pictographs without the pictures. They take less time, not to mention a slightly depleted imagination. Regardless, these graphs are valuable for quick reference and easy comparison.

The Experiment

Density is a word that describes how tightly packed the atoms inside a material are. For example, if you were to take two rocks, pumice and granite, you would find that they are made out of exactly the same mix of minerals. They are identical, except that the granite was formed when a big blob of molten rock cooled very slowly underground, and the pumice was formed when the exact same molten mass of rock was spit out of a volcano. If you placed both rocks in water, the granite would sink and the pumice would float. The granite is denser, or packed tighter together, than the pumice.

Another way to explore this idea is using liquids. All liquids have different densities. If you could shrink down to the size of an atom and could swim around inside a glass of water and a glass of corn syrup, you could compare which one was more crowded. Chances are the corn syrup would win that contest. The lab you are about to do will allow you to compare the different densities of five liquids.

Materials

1 Triple beam balance (if available)
1 50 mL Beaker
50 mL Water
50 mL Rubbing alcohol
50 mL Glycerine
50 mL Corn syrup
50 mL Cooking oil

Procedure

1. Zero out your triple beam balance.

2. Once you are certain that your balance is calibrated, take a 50 mL beaker and place it on the scale. Weigh the beaker and enter that weight into the column on the data table that is labeled Weight of Beaker (g). If you don't have a balance the typical weight of a beaker is 100 g.

Timeline

25-30 minutes

Vocabulary Builder

7. Bar Graph

A picture of the data that has been collected represented as a circle or pie cut into portions. Each portion represents a group of the data collected.

8. Constant

This is the column header that is measured in regular intervals, time is a good example.

9. Variable

This is the data you are after, the information that you want to collect, it is unpredictable and varies widely.

10. Unit

How you measure the constant and varible. The units can be degrees celcius, meters, grams, milliliters, or anything else. The units are listed next to the variable or contant in parenthesis.

11. Ordered Pairs

Every set of numbers in a data table is an ordered pair. These pairs are really easy to pick out because they are either side by side or one atop the other.

Bar Graph • Liquid Densities

3. Add 50 mL of water to the 50 mL beaker and place it onto the scale. Determine the weight of the beaker with the water in it and enter that number into the column labeled Beaker + Liquid (g).

4. Repeat this process with the other four liquids. Again, if you do not have a triple beam balance the following weights would be representative of the liquids used in this lab. Water = 50g, Corn Syrup = 46 g. Alcohol= 52 g, Glycerine= 60 g, Cooking Oil= 42 g

5. When you have finished weighing the five liquids, determine the net weight of each liquid by subracting the weight of the empty beaker from the weight of the beaker with the liquid in it:

Gross Weight	Beaker with liquid
	– <u>Beaker empty</u>
Net Weight	Weight of liquid

6. Calculate the density of each liquid using the formula, density = mass/volume. You just calculated the mass of each liquid sample in Step 5 and you know that you used 50 mL of liquid each time. The quick way to do this is …

Density of Liquid = Mass of Liquid (g)/50 mL

Data Table

Fill in each of the columns in this data table as you complete the steps in the experiment.

Relative Densities of Common Liquids

Liquid (50 mL)	Weight of Beaker (g)	Beaker + Liquid (g)	Net Weight (g)	Density (g/mL)
Water				
Corn Syrup				
Alcohol				
Glycerine				
Cooking Oil				

Creating a Bar Graph

A complete bar graph has eight characteristics:

A. A vertical line, near the left hand side of the paper, drawn with a ruler.
B. A horizontal line near the bottom of the page, drawn with a ruler.
C. A descriptive title at the top of the page.
D. A constant (uniform standard of measure) listed under the horizontal axis.
E. A variable describing what information is to be collected during the experiment, listed along the vertical axis.
F. Units identifying how the variable and constant were measured.
G. Data that has been collected in ordered pairs.
H. All data presented as neat, little boxes or vertical columns.

Using the information from the data table on the previous page, fill in the blanks:

Title: ______________________________________

Constant: Type of Liquid

Variable: __________________________________

Unit used: grams

Data Collected

Density of Water: 1.0 g/mL

Density of Corn Syrup: _________ g/mL

Density of Alcohol: _________ g/mL

Density of Glycerine: _________ g/mL

Density of Cooking Oil: _________ g/mL

Step 1: Draw the horizontal and vertical axis. Use a ruler.

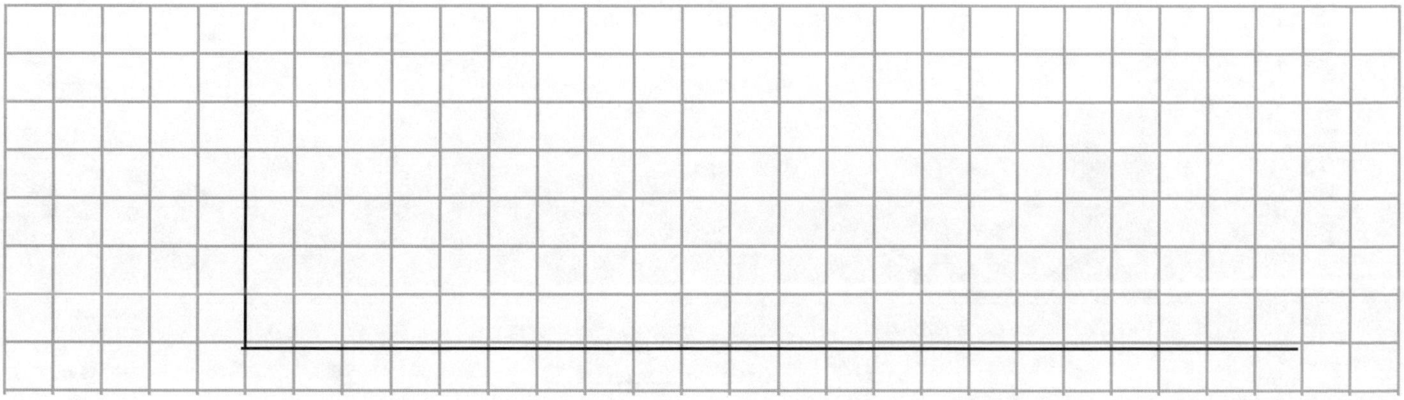

Bar Graph • Liquid Densities

Step 2: Label the horizontal and vertical axis with the constant and variable.

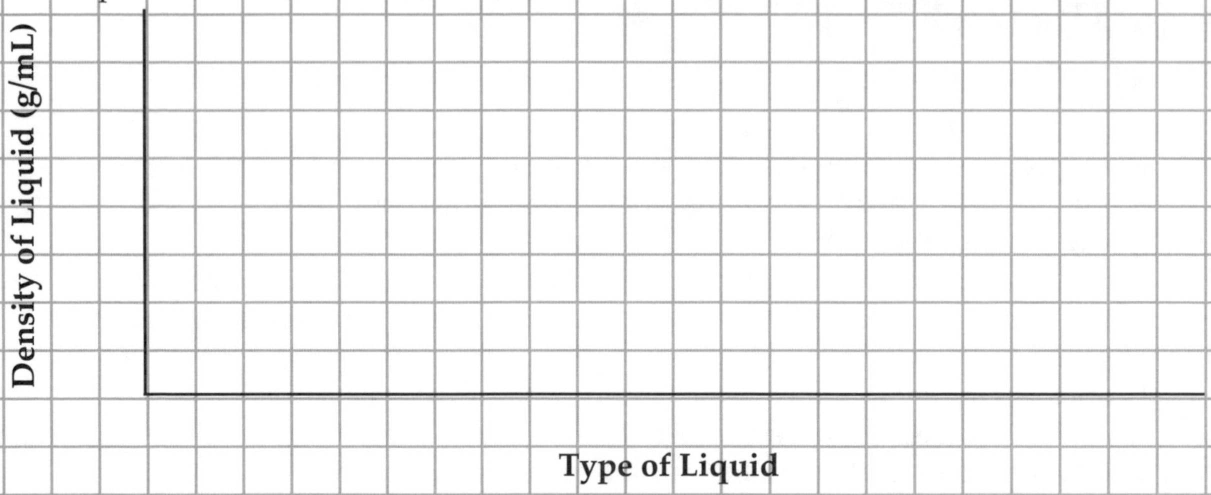

Step 3: Calibrate (add numbers or names) to both axes.

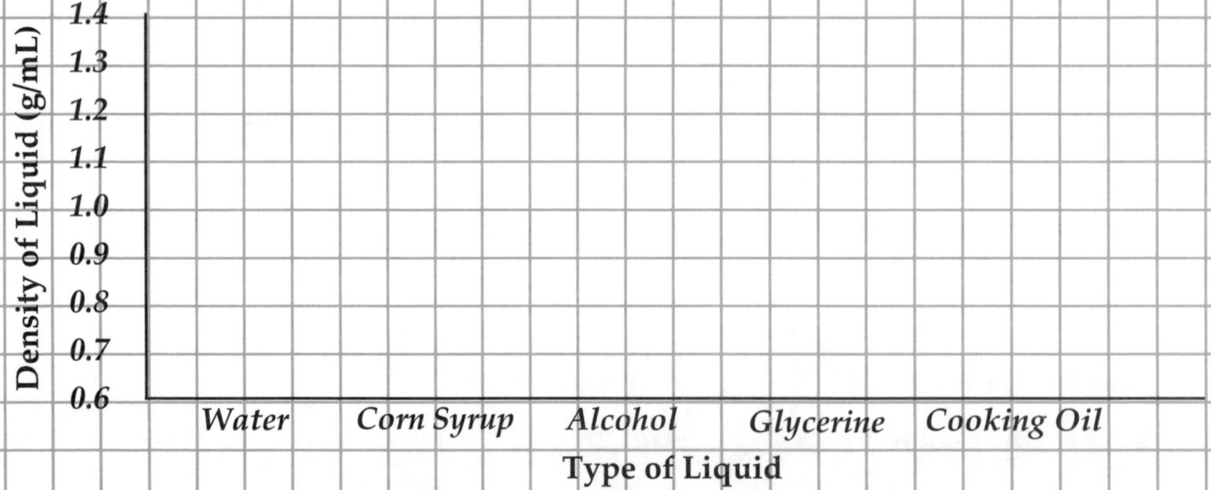

Step 4: Plot your first liquid (water) and draw a box. Color the box solid.

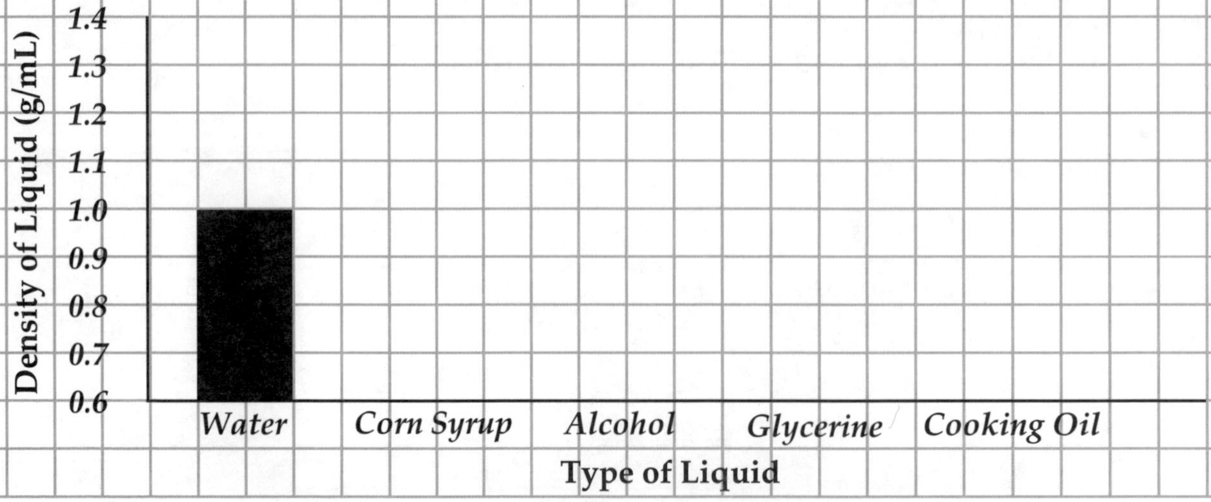

Bar Graph • Liquid Densities

Name: ______________________ Assignment #5 Due: __________

Teacher: ______________________ Period: ________ Score: ____ / 40 pts

Complete the bar graph comparing liquid densities in the space provided below.

Learning to Speak Line Graph

The Parts of a Graph

Axes (lines)

There are actually two lines—nothing fancy, no wiggles, no abstract, counterintuitive, neo–Scibbilian extracts. Just two straight lines, one going across the bottom of the page and another going up the side of the page.

A. The Horizontal Axis. This is the line that zips across the bottom of the page. It is one of the anchors for a good graph. If you have a tough time remembering which way horizontal goes, just shorten the word to horizon. Horizons are relatively level and run from left to right, separating the sky from the land.

B. The Vertical Axis. This is the line that zips up the left-hand side of the page. It is the other anchor for the graph.

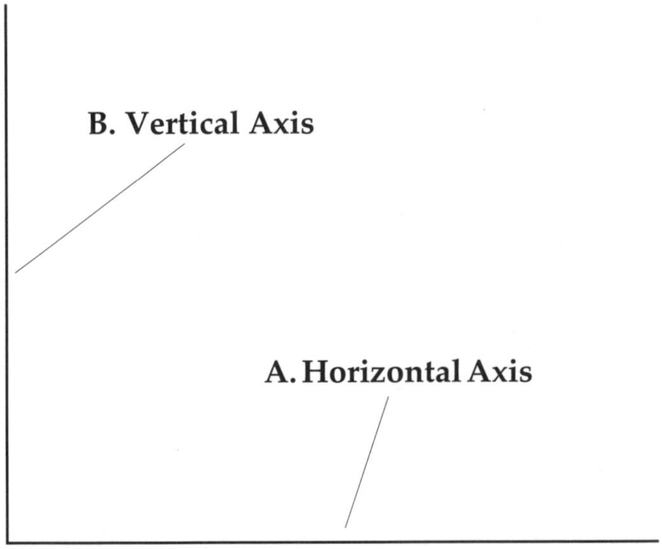

Line ID

OK, so you have these two lines. Big deal, what do they mean? Each line has a purpose. The bottom line is the home for the constant, and the vertical line is the home for the variable.

A. Constant. Just like the name suggests, this is the thing that you measure with regularity. It is predictable, it is measured at even intervals, and it forms the foundation for the experiment. Constants are things such as measuring the time every minute or increasing the weight by ten grams each trial. Constants are known going into the experiment and can be entered into data tables before the lab begins. It is always listed on the bottom, horizontal axis.

B. Variable. This is the thing that you are measuring. It changes, it is unpredictable, it is what you want to know about the experiment. Some examples of variables are how does the temperature change, does the speed increase, and what happens to the brightness of the bulb? It is always listed on the side, vertical axis.

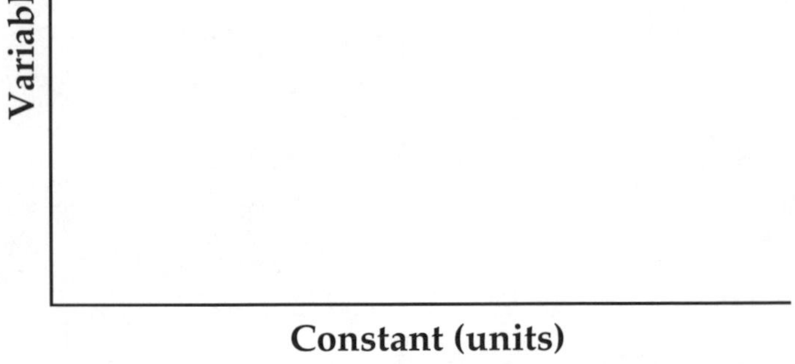

More Line ID

Things are looking up. You have two lines. You know that the horizontal axis is your constant and the vertical axis is your variable. Unfortunately, we are still missing a bit of information.

A. Units. How do you plan to measure the constant and variable—degrees Celsius, minutes, millimeters, pints, or what? What do those numbers mean along those axes? Both the constant and the variable need to be accompanied by the units that they are measured in. Without this information, the data is worthless.

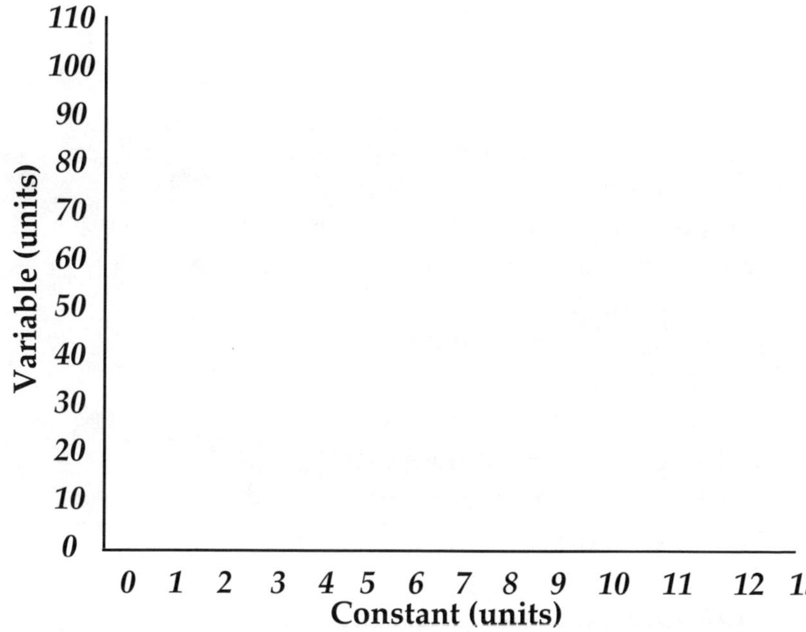

B. Numerical Increments. This is a fancy term that means that you need to add numbers to identify the lines in the graph. *The numbers that you use will be determined by the constant and the data that you collect.*

The Guts

Your graph is set up. Now all you have to do is take the data in the data table and make a picture from it. That is exactly what a graph is—a picture of the data in the data table.

A. Ordered Pairs. The data is usually collected in ordered pairs. For example, if you were heating water, your data table may read that at ten minutes (the constant), the temperature of the water might be 64° Celsius (the variable).

Find the 10-minute mark on the horizontal axis and trace an imaginary line straight up. Find the 64° line on the vertical axis and trace an imaginary line straight across. Where the two lines intersect is the data point for that ordered pair. You have just plotted a piece of the picture.

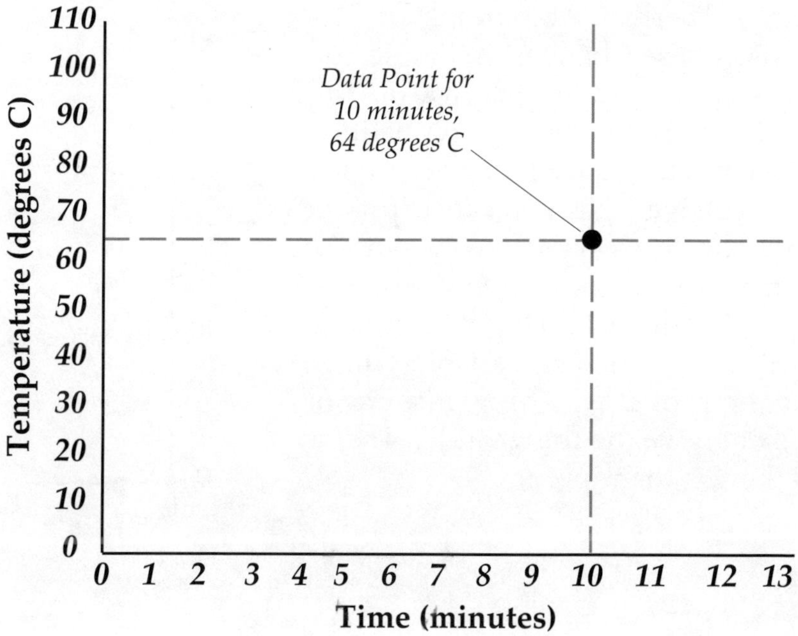

Learning to Speak Line Graph

B. Data Points. You don't stop with a single set of ordered pairs. You have an entire picture to draw, so you need to enter all of the ordered pairs that you collected onto the graph as data points. When you are finished, your work could look something like this if you are heating water.

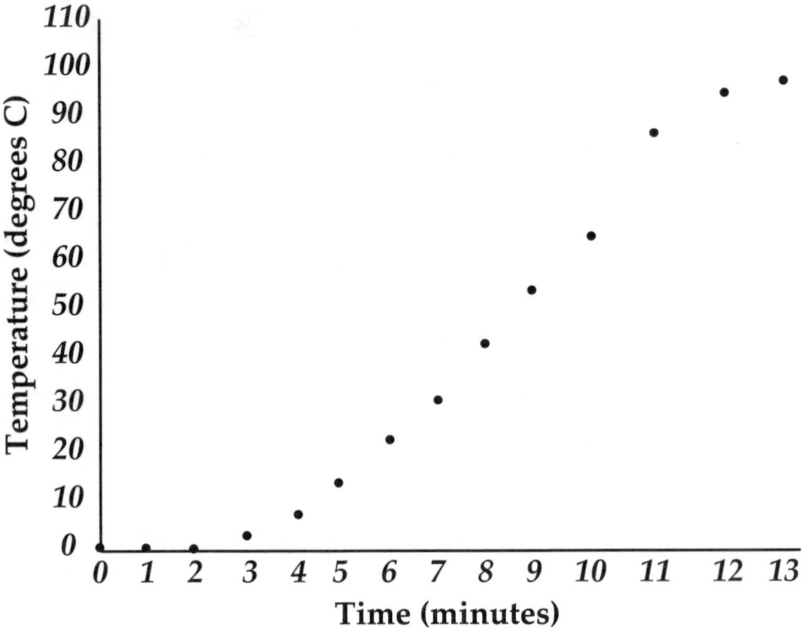

C. Bars or Lines. Once you have all of your data points plotted, then it is time for you to add bars if this is a bar graph, or lines if this is a line or a best fit graph. We are going to assume, for this example, that you are interested in presenting your data as a line graph. Once you get all of the ordered pairs plotted as data points onto the graph, nab your ruler, sharpen your pencil, and play dot-to-dot. The almost-finished product will look something like this …

The Title

The finishing touch is the title, which tells just exactly what it is that all these numbers and lines mean. Don't be too clever or fancy; this is one place where you don't get points for being creative. The title, Heating of Ice Water, is quick, concise, and to-the-point. Thermal Accounting of Molecular Phase Changes in Simple Solvents sure sounds impressive, but unless you are a finalist in a competition for "Synaptic Whiz of the Year," it is a bit excessive. No need to trip over your shoelaces on the way out the door to recess.

So, that's it. Draw a couple of lines. Add numbers, variables, units, and a pile of dots. Throw in a line or two and give the thing a title. That is all there is to graphing.

Heating of Ice Water

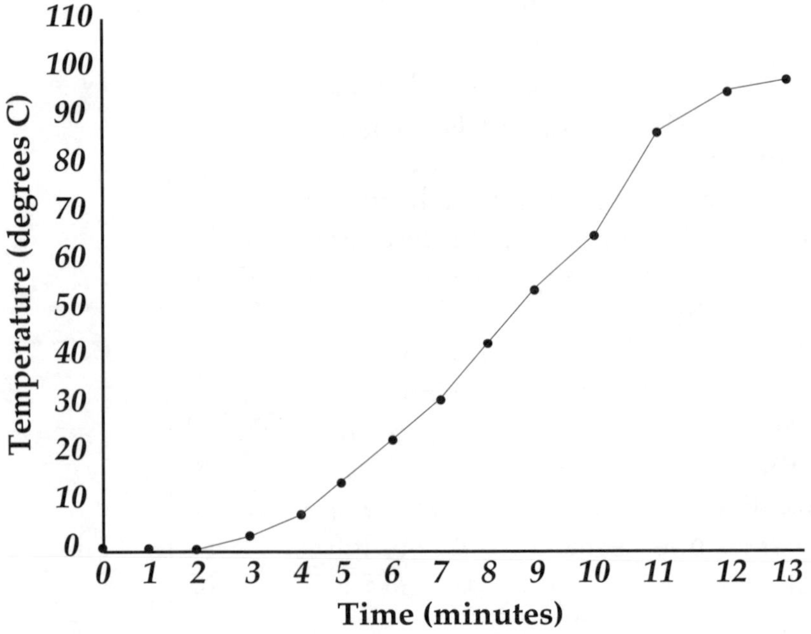

Line Graphs in Reverse

Name: ______________________ Assignment #6 Due: __________

Teacher: ______________________ Period: ________ Score: ____ / 24 pts

1. Using the line graph at the bottom of page 34, fill in the spaces below.

   A. Title: ______________________________________

   B. Constant: ______________________________________

   C. Unit for Contant: ______________________________________

   D. Variable: ______________________________________

   E. Unit for Variable: ______________________________________

   F. Ordered Pairs: ______, ______ ______, ______

   ______, ______ ______, ______

   ______, ______ ______, ______

   ______, ______ ______, ______

   ______, ______ ______, ______

   ______, ______ ______, ______

   ______, ______ ______, ______

2. Construct a data table from the information that you have collected.

Instant Handwarmer

Timeline
25-30 minutes

Vocabulary Builder
12. Horizontal Axis

The line running along the bottom of the graph. This is the home for the constant.

13. Vertical Axis

The line running along the left hand side of the graph. This is the home for the variable.

14. Line Graph

A picture of the data collected in a data table represented as a series of dots, plotted from the ordered pairs, connected with a straight line going from dot to dot.

Concepts
Single Variable Data Table
Line Graph

Single Variable Data Table
Single variable data tables are set up to record a single variable against a constant. These data tables have two columns, one for the variable and one for the constant. They can run either horizontally or vertically.

The Experiment
Two chemicals will be mixed in a sealed container. When the gas pressure increases to the point where the container fails, we will have a small and very polite explosion of gas.

Materials
1 Beaker, 250 mL
1 Thermometer, °C/°F
1 Calcium chloride, 1 oz.
1 Resealable baggie
Water

Procedure
1. Using the beaker, measure out 150 mL of warm water. Add that 150 mL of water to the baggie. If you don't have a measuring cup, fill the bag until there is about an inch of water in it. **(Be sure to use warm water. Using cold water will change the experiment significantly.)**

2. Place the thermometer in the water and take an initial reading. Enter that number into the data table on the next page.

3. Remove the cap from the calcium chloride bottle and add four caps of calcium chloride to the water. Insert the thermometer and zip the baggie closed. As the chemical starts to dissolve, you should notice a significant increase in temperature. Record the temperature every minute for 10 minutes.

Data & Observations

1. Using the data that you collected, fill in the spaces below. Come up with your own title.

A. Title: ______________________________

B. Constant: ______________________________

C. Unit for Constant: ______________________________

D. Variable: ______________________________

E. Unit for Variable: ______________________________

F. Ordered Pairs: ______, ______ ______, ______

______, ______ ______, ______ ______, ______

______, ______ ______, ______ ______, ______

______, ______ ______, ______ ______, ______

2. Construct a data table in the space below, to represent the data above.

How Come, Huh?

When calcium chloride is mixed with water, it splits apart, forming calcium ions and chloride ions. When this happens, the energy that was holding those atoms together is released as heat. That is why the bag started to feel warm as the reaction proceeded.

Instant Handwarmer

Name :______________________________ Assignment #7 Due: ____________

Teacher: _____________________________ Period: __________ Score: ____ / 56 pts

Using the data from the data table on page 37, construct a line graph.

Pendulum Puzzles

The Experiment

You have a pendulum made out of string, a paper clip, and a couple of washers. The pendulum works just fine, but you want it to swing a little bit faster. Do you add more weight to your pendulum, lengthen the string, shorten the string, or pull the pendulum back farther so that it has more energy? Answers, please. We are all breathless in anticipation.

Materials

1 String, 90 cm long
1 Metric meterstick
1 Paper clip
3 Washers, 1.5-inch diameter
1 Hand
Gravity

Procedure

1. Now we are going to study pendulums. There are two things that actually may affect how long it takes a pendulum to swing back and forth—the length of the pendulum and the weight of the pendulum. We are going to experiment with both. First we need to have a few rules:

a. You will always time the swings for 30 seconds.

b. You will always release the pendulum from the same place. Don't release it farther back one time and closer another.

c. You will count once each time the pendulum passes your belly button.

2. To make your pendulum, you will need to bend the paper clip out into an "S" shape. Tie one end onto the string and add washers to the other end. Use the illustration shown here as a guide.

3. With the assistance of your teacher or parents, fill in the chart on the next page. To get you started, the first experiment is like this. You will put one washer on the paper clip and hold the string at a height of 30 cm. Let it swing for 30 seconds and record the number of swings in the box under 1 and next to 30 cm.

Timeline

35-40 minutes

Vocabulary Builder

15. Multiple Line Graph

A picture of the data collected in a data table represented as a series of dots, plotted from the ordered pairs, connected with a straight line going from dot to dot.

Concepts

Multiple Data Tables
Multiple Line Graphs

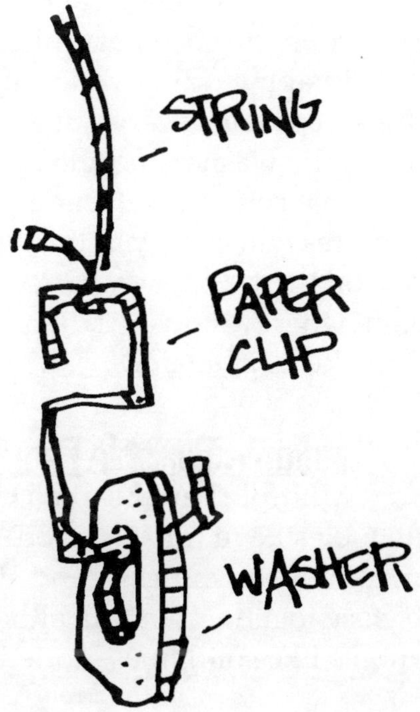

Pendulum Puzzles

4. Now add a second washer and count for another 30 seconds; record your answer under 2 washers in the 30 cm row.

5. Finally, add a third washer and repeat the procedure.

6. Repeat this experimental sequence using a pendulum that is 45 cm, 60 cm, 75 cm, and 90 cm long. Record your data in the space provided on the next page.

7. When you are done collecting data set up your data table on page 42. The horizontal line will be the weight of the washers: 1, 2, or 3. The vertical axis will be the length of the strings in cm.

8. Plot each string, one at a time, using a different colored pencil. When you are all done you will be able to look at the multiple line graph and evaluate a lot of data at the same time.

How Come, Huh?

As you should be able to see from your data, the only thing that really matters in this experiment is the length of the string. The mass and the distance that you pull the string back have no effect on the speed at which the pendulum swings.

Imagine riding your bike down a hill, into a dip, and back up again. If the dip is little (short string), your trip is very quick. If the dip is large (long string), your trip is going to take a while. The mass of the washer and the amount of potential energy has no influence.

In terms of kinetic and potential energy, the pendulum gets its initial energy from your hand and stores that energy at the top of the swing. As the pendulum swings, it uses the stored energy to move on the way down. Once it passes the center point, it starts to store energy again until it gets to a point where it stops. At this point, it is full of potential energy. Gravity starts to pull on it, and kinetic energy kicks in again.

Multiple Variable Data Tables

Multiple variable data tables are set up to record several variables against a constant. These data tables have three or more columns for the variables and one for the constant. They run either horizontally or vertically and allow you to compare different conditions at the same time. If the lines are close together you can either use different colors to depict the different variables or you can use symbols like solid lines, dotted lines, dashed line, etc.

Pendulum Puzzles

Name: ______________________ Assignment #8 Due: __________

Teacher: ______________________ Period: ________ Score: ____ / 55 pts

Data Table Construction

This kind of data table allows you to invoke the multiple variable clause into your contract. We are going to use the title *Pendulum Puzzles*—simple, to the point, and lets readers know what they are looking at. The constant in this lab is the mass (measured in number of washers), and the variables are the length of the strings (measured in centimeters). You will collect the ordered pairs and, at this point in your education, you should be able to complete this assignment without a hitch. Time to fill in the data table …

Counting Pendulum Swings

Mass (# Washers)	1	2	3
String # 1 (30 cm)			
String # 2 (45 cm)			
String # 3 (60 cm)			
String # 4 (75 cm)			
String # 5 (90 cm)			

Multiple Variable Line Graphs

Imagine taking the data from 5 different experiments, 5 different data tables, and plopping them all on a single graph where they overlap. That is what is called a multiple variable line graph. You are going to take the data from the table above and plot it on the graph paper on the next page. The main difference is that you are going to use a different colored pencil for each of the variables (strings for this lab). Make a color key at the bottom of the next page for reference.

Pendulum Puzzles

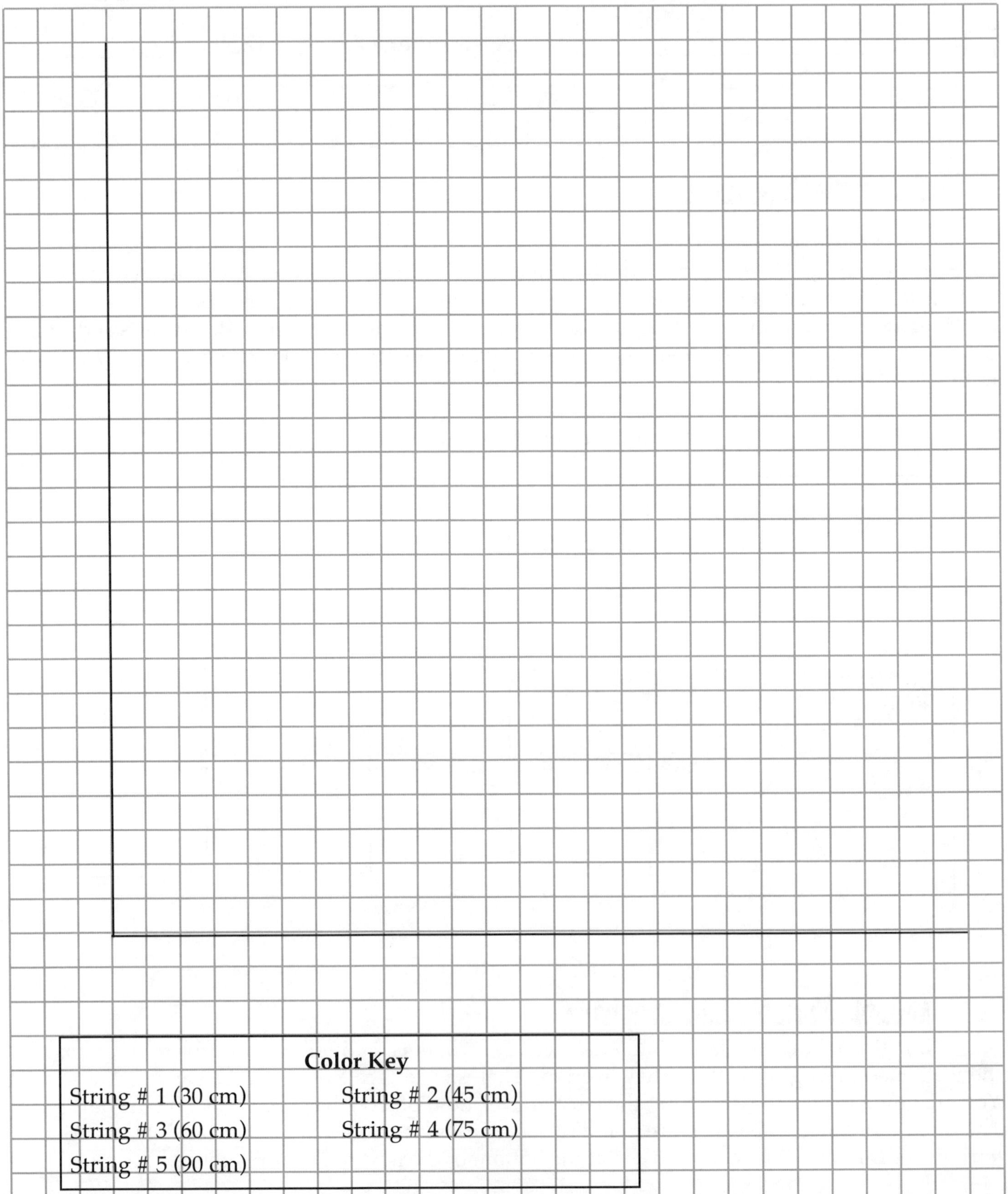

Vocabuary Quiz

Name: ______________________	Assignment #9	Due: __________
Teacher: ______________________	Period: ________	Score: ____ / 50 pts

A. Fill in the blanks with the correct word or words. 2 points/blank, 10 points.

1. How you measure the constant and varible. The __________ can be degrees celcius, meters, grams, milliliters, or anything else. They are listed next to the variable or constant in parenthesis.

2. Every set of numbers in a data table is an ______________________. These are really easy to pick out because they are either side by side or one atop the other.

3. A series of boxes that are used to organize the data collected during the lab activity. A complete ______________________ has a title, constant and variable with units in parenthesis, and information collected and recorded as ordered pairs.

4. The line running along the bottom of the graph is called the ________________ axis. This is the home for the constant.

5. A ______________________ is a picture of the data collected in a data table represented as a series of dots, plotted from the ordered pairs, connected with a straight line going from dot to dot.

B. Answer the questions below.

1. Name the four kinds of graphs you learned to create. 2 points/answer, 8 points

A. ______________________ C. ______________________

B. ______________________ D. ______________________

2. List the eight parts of a line graph. 1 point/answer, 8 points

A. ______________________ E. ______________________

B. ______________________ F. ______________________

C. ______________________ G. ______________________

D. ______________________ H. ______________________

Vocabuary Quiz

B. Match words with definitions. Write the number of the word on the line next to the definition that most closely describes that word. *There are more words than there are defintions.* 2 points / correct blank, 24 points.

1. *Data*
2. *Quantitaive Measurement*
3. *Data Table*
4. *Title*
5. *Column Header*
6. *Pie Graph*
7. *Constant*
8. *Variable*
9. *Unit*
10. *Ordered Pairs*
11. *Data Table*
12. *Horizontal Axis*
13. *Vertical Axis*
14. *Line Graph*
15. *Multiple Line Graphs*

____ A picture of the data collected in a data table represented as a series of dots, plotted from the ordered pairs, connected with a straight line going from dot to dot.

____ Information that you collect during your lab experiments.

____ A picture of the data that has been collected represented as a circle or pie cut into portions. Each portion represents a group of the data collected.

____ This is the column header that is measured in regular intervals, time is a good example.

____ The line running along the left hand side of the graph. This is the home for the variable.

____ This is the data you are after, the information that you want to collect. It is unpredictable and varies widely.

____ How you measure the constant and varible. They can be degrees celcius, meters, grams, milliliters, or anything else. They are listed next to the variable or contant in parenthesis.

____ Every set of numbers in a data table. They are really easy to pick out because they are either side by side or one atop the other.

____ An organized box where you enter the data that you collect during the experiment.

____ The collection of data using calibrated instruments like beakers, rulers, and balances.

____ The line running along the bottom of the graph. This is the home for the constant.

____ A word or words that describes the data recorded in the data table.

Final Quiz • Graphing

Name: ______________________ Assignment #10 Pages 1, 2 of 4

Teacher: ______________________ Period: ________ Score: ____ / 100 pts

Heating of Ice Water

Time (minutes)	0	2	4	6	8	10	12	14	16	18	20	22	24
Temp. (°C)	0	0	0	4	16	28	42	56	68	81	96	100	100

1. Using the data table above, fill in the spaces below. (15 points/1 pt each blank)

A. Title: ______________________________________

B. Constant: ______________________________________

C. Unit for Contant: ______________________________________

D. Variable: ______________________________________

E. Unit for Variable: ______________________________________

F. Ordered Pairs: 6 minutes, ________ ________, 0 °C

________, 42 °C 10 minutes, ________

________, 96 °C 18 minutes, ________

G. The coolest temperature for the water reading was __________.

H How long did it take for the water to boil? (100°C) __________.

I. The temperature of the water was taken every _______ minutes.

J. The coldest temperature reading was ________.

2. Use the data below and construct a data table on the graph paper above. (20 points/2 pts each item: title, varibles, units, and each ordered pair). *Don't forget your boxes.*

A. Cooling of Molten Sulfur to a Solid

B. Time in minutes is listed below

0 min, 10 min, 20 min, 30 min, 40 min,

C. Temperature measured in degrees celcius is listed below

180° C, 163 ° C, 135 ° C, 86° C, 53 ° C

3. Using the data table above, fill in the spaces below. (15 points/1 pt each blank)

A. Title: ____

B. Constant: ____

C. Unit for Contant: ____________________________________

D. Variable: ____

E. Unit for Variable: ____________________________________

F. Ordered Pairs: ________, ________ ________, ________

________, ________ ________, ________

________, ________

G. In this experiment the sulfur is changing from a ___________ to a ___________.

H. The experiment lasted for a total of ____ minutes, measured every ____ minutes.

I. The highest temperature recorded was _____ ° C.

Name ____________________________________ Final Quiz • Pages 3, 4 of 4

4. Construct a line graph from the information in question 2. (26 points)

2 points for the title	2 points for a neat, horizontal line
2 points for a neat, vertical line	2 points for the variable
2 points for the constant	2 points for each unit (4 pts)
2 points for ordered pairs (10 points)	2 points for a neat line

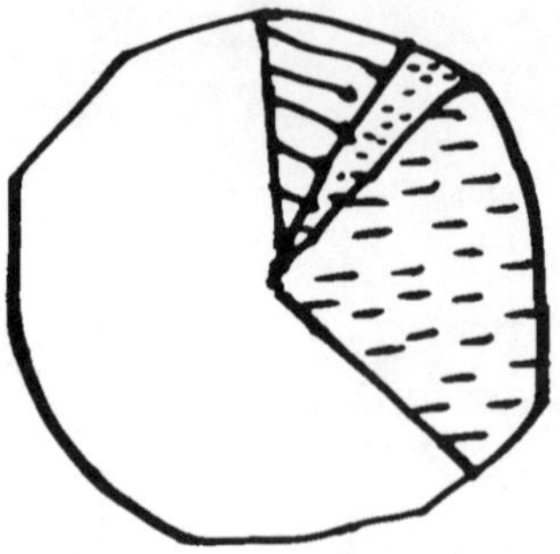

A.

B.

C.

5. Answer the following questions using the three graphs above. (24 points; 2 pts each blank))

A. Write the names of the three graphs next to the corresponding letter.

A. ______________________________

B. ______________________________

C. ______________________________

B. Which graph is usually used in association with a tabulation data table? ______.

C. Which graph would probably have 10 sets of ordered pairs? _____.

D. Which graph is best for showing percentages of a whole? _____.

E. How many different choices were graphed in Graph A? _____.

F. Which graph would be considered a bar graph? _____.

G. Which graph appears to show an increase? _____.

H. Which graph is a multiple line graph? _____________.

6. Sign your name on the line below and write today's date. (2 points)

____ ___________